E3 CALL HOME

*For the shorebirds and especially, of course, E3.
Long may they fly.*

A catalogue record for this book is available from the National Library of New Zealand

A RANDOM HOUSE BOOK
published by Random House New Zealand
18 Poland Road, Glenfield, Auckland, New Zealand
For more information on our titles go to www.randomhouse.co.nz

Random House New Zealand is part of the Random House Group
New York   London   Sydney   Auckland   Delhi   Johannesburg

First published 2009. Reprinted 2010.

© 2009 Janet Hunt

The moral rights of the author have been asserted

ISBN 978 1 86979 276 3

This book is copyright. Except for the purposes of fair reviewing no part of this publication may be reproduced or transmitted in any form or by any means, electronic or mechanical, including photocopying, recording or any information storage and retrieval system, without permission in writing from the publisher.

Unless otherwise credited, illustrations and photographs by Janet Hunt.
Worms, shells and crabs illustration page 4 from *Life in the Estuary: Illustrated Guide and Ecology* by Malcolm B Jones and Islay D Marsden, courtesy of the authors; birds in illustrations pages 22 and 27 from a photograph by Jesse Conklin; spoon-billed sandpiper page 28 courtesy of Nial Moores. All other photographs are credited on the pages where they are used.

Design: Janet Hunt
Printed in China through Bookbuilders

E3 CALL HOME

JANET HUNT

RANDOM HOUSE
NEW ZEALAND

It was late March, 2007. High above the Pacific Ocean, far from land, a small grey and white striped bird with an extremely long bill and a handsome, copper-coloured chest was in trouble. He was a godwit, and his name was E3.

No matter how hard he flew, he could not keep up with the other birds in his flock. He was almost exhausted.

If he didn't find somewhere to rest very soon, he would slowly fall lower and lower.

He would tumble from the sky into the sea.

He would drown.

E3 is an eastern bar-tailed godwit. His Maori name is kūaka. His scientific name is *Limosa lapponica baueri*.

He is a wading bird, a bird with long legs that finds its food in watery places like tidal flats.

Photo: Dorothy Pashniak

E3 was flying from the bottom of the world to the top — from New Zealand to Alaska, a distance of around 17,000 kilometres depending on the route. Even if he was going to take at least one break along the way, that's an extraordinarily long way for a bird who is only about 39 centimetres from the tip of his 10 centimetre bill to the end of his stubby tail.

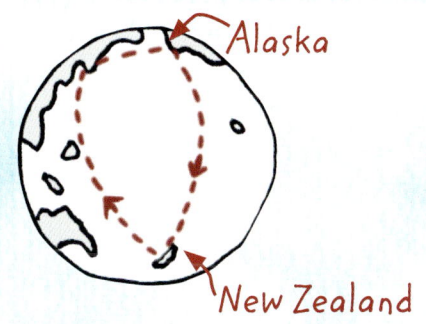

E3's story began late in the afternoon about a month earlier. He was minding his own business on the muddy-sandy-watery seashore at Miranda on the east coast of the North Island of New Zealand. He was just an ordinary godwit then, no different from any other.

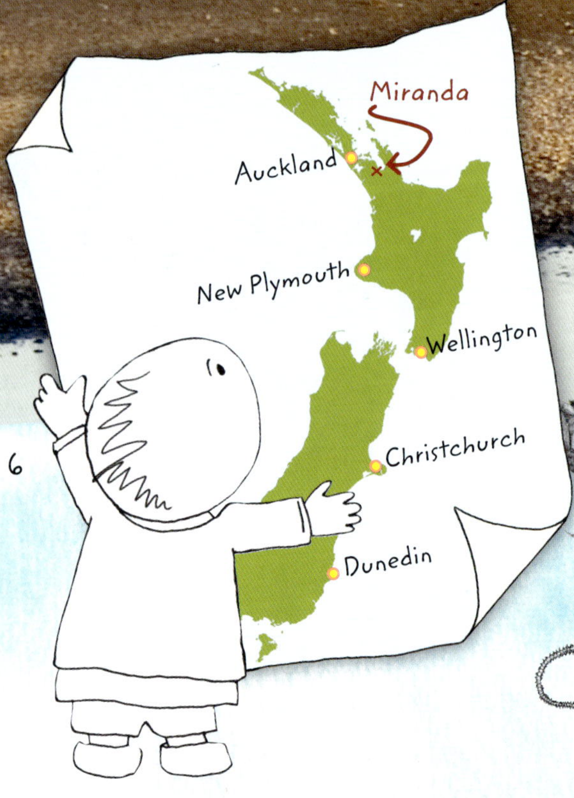

Miranda is a giant seabird supermarket filled with all the things a shorebird could want — tiny shellfish and crabs and most of all, many species of marine worm.

The day had been hot and the sun was low in the sky. The mud crackled and popped.

E3 was eating like a pig, scoffing skinny hairy worms and crackly shrimps and crunchy crabs and tiny tasty shellfish. Sometimes he poked his long, narrow bill so deep in the mud he was almost up to his eyeballs.

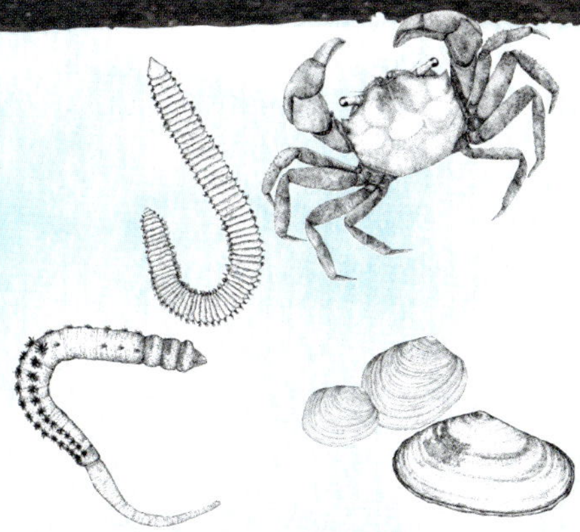

Godwit bills have touchy-feely, flexible tips (like this yawning female's) to catch those good things deep in the mud.

Females have longer bills than males, which means they eat slightly different food. That way there is enough for everyone.

The tide was coming in. Small waves jostled and pushed and ran over one another, each a tiny bit closer to the shore than the one before.

At first the water washed around E3's ankles and then it swished behind his knees. At last it bumped and sloshed at his bottom.

When it became too deep he flapped his wings and gave a little jump over the heads of the other godwits.

He splashed into the shallow water behind them, then carried right on feeding. He needed to eat as much as he could.

Godwits are not like ducks or gulls. Ducks and gulls have webbed feet and waterproof feathers. They float like corks and paddle like rowing boats.

Wading birds like E3 have long toes that are excellent for picking through mud, but not much use for swimming, and their feathers are only slightly waterproof. They can't really float.

Why do some godwits have orange-red chest feathers but others don't?

It makes them look sexy. In February and March when the birds are preparing for nesting, they change into their brightest feathers (males especially). For the rest of the year, godwits' feathers are pale grey-brown and white.

Godwits are not the only birds that wear breeding plumage. This New Zealand dotterel looked very handsome when it was breeding in spring on a shellbank on Waiheke Island.

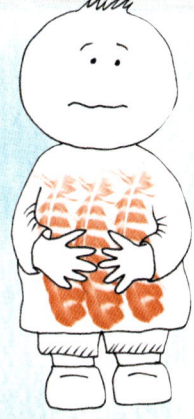

Right along the shore, thousands of birds just like E3 were feeding, scratching and preening their feathers. It was almost time to fly to the stilt pools in the paddock behind the beach. They would tuck their bills into their feathers, hoist one leg up, and snooze until the tide went out again.

Among the other wading birds on the shore there were red knots, New Zealand dotterels, two kinds of oystercatcher, white-faced herons, pied stilts and wrybills.

Here they are, from tallest to smallest.

White-faced heron

Variable oystercatcher

Pied oystercatcher

They didn't know about the trap that was waiting for them.

Eyes followed their every move. Men and women with binoculars and telescopes watched the birds like hungry cats from beside a hide in the paddock.

They were scientists and their helpers.

"Not long now," said their leader, a man named Phil.

The others nodded. They were tense.

But they were ready.

Early morning is a good time to watch land birds, but waders are more in tune with the tide than with the sun. They are best seen when they come inshore to roost. Wait for them to come to you. Be very still and quiet. Birds have good eyesight and good hearing (but not much sense of smell).

Binoculars and telescopes ('scopes) are great for getting up close and a field guide helps identify what you are seeing.

Write down: • kind of bird • when seen • where • how many there were (guesstimate). Make sketches of interesting things and above all . . .

DO NOT DISTURB

As soon as the tide was full the birds began to fly inland.
E3 circled over the sea, then headed towards the pools.
They gleamed ahead of him in the evening light.

When 2 - 1 = 0
(or how to fool a bird).
Most birds can't count! If two people go into a hide (the shed in the picture on page 12 is a hide) and then one leaves, birds think the hide is empty. Keen birders sometimes use this trick to get close to birds they want to watch.

Make a list of all the species of birds you have ever seen. (This is called a 'life list'.) You may be surprised by how many you know.

BOOF! He collided with a fine black mesh, like a giant spider web. It was a mist net.

14

Mist nets are hung between two bamboo poles. They are made of fine black nylon mesh with net pouches to catch the birds, and are almost invisible in the early evening. E3 had to be freed quickly or he would harm himself struggling to escape.

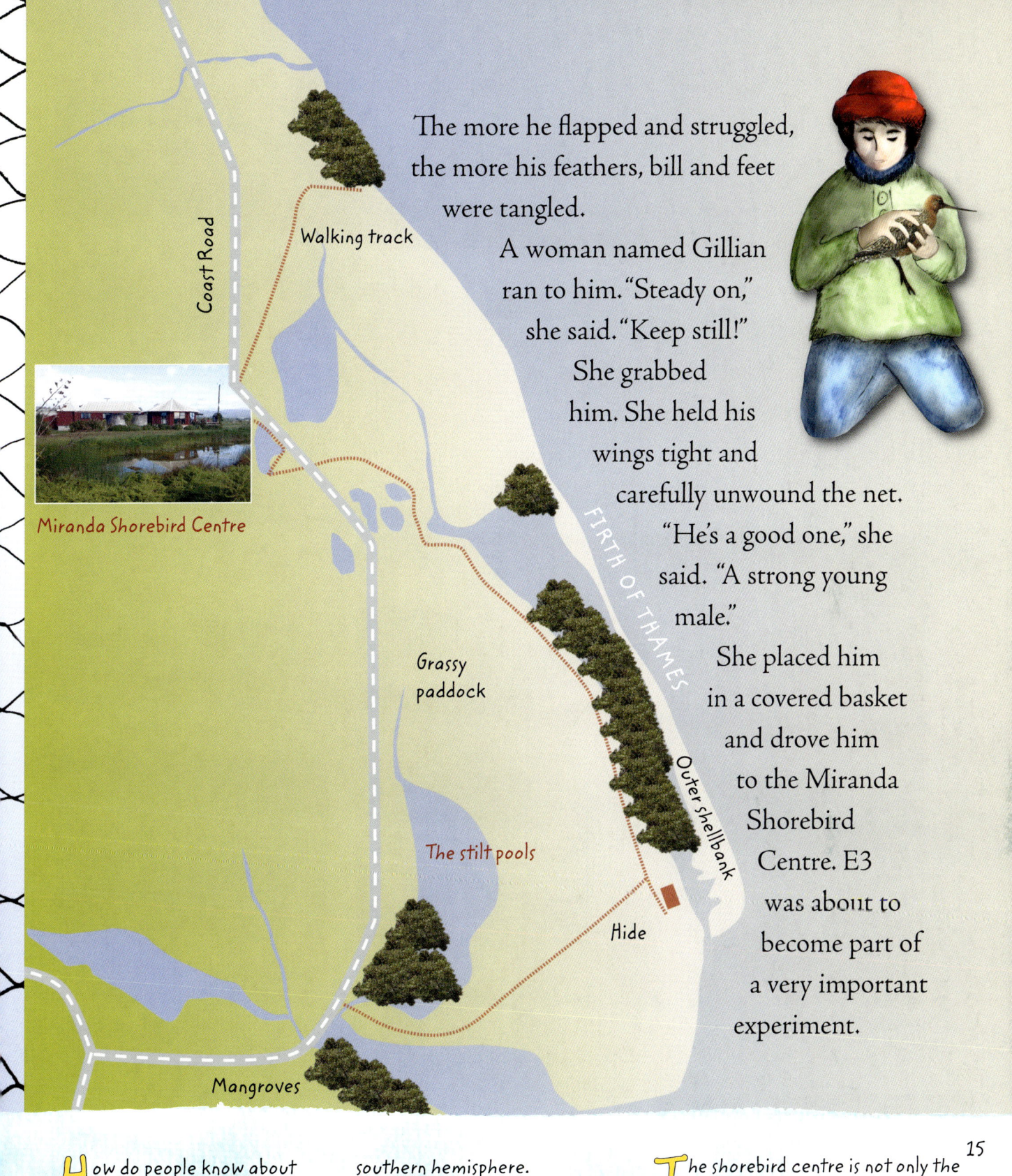

The more he flapped and struggled, the more his feathers, bill and feet were tangled.

A woman named Gillian ran to him. "Steady on," she said. "Keep still!" She grabbed him. She held his wings tight and carefully unwound the net. "He's a good one," she said. "A strong young male."

She placed him in a covered basket and drove him to the Miranda Shorebird Centre. E3 was about to become part of a very important experiment.

How do people know about migratory birds?

Adult godwits are mainly seen in the far north of many lands in the northern spring but then they disappear. They turn up in the southern spring and summer around the coasts of lands in the southern hemisphere.

But are they the same birds? How do they get from one place to another?

Researchers had puzzled over these questions for a long time, and E3 was going to help find the answers.

The shorebird centre is not only the HQ of the Miranda Naturalists' Trust, it is also a vital link in an international network dedicated to the protection of migratory shore birds.

At the centre E3 was turned this way and that. His feathers were examined and counted, his bill was measured and he was weighed. He was frightened but not hurt.

An identity band was clipped on his right leg and a small black flag that said **E3** was clipped on his left.

Finally, a tiny solar-powered transmitter was attached to his back by a harness looped around his legs. His photo was taken and he was placed back in the basket.

The birder's grip is a means of holding a bird safely.

This male godwit's feathers are being checked for wear.

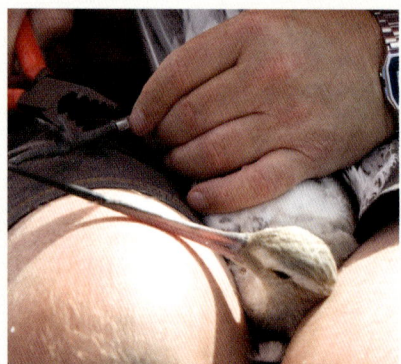

This female is having an ID band clipped on her leg.

Biologist Nils Warnock is holding E3. Keith Woodley, the manager of the Miranda Shorebird Centre, is recording the bird's vital statistics.

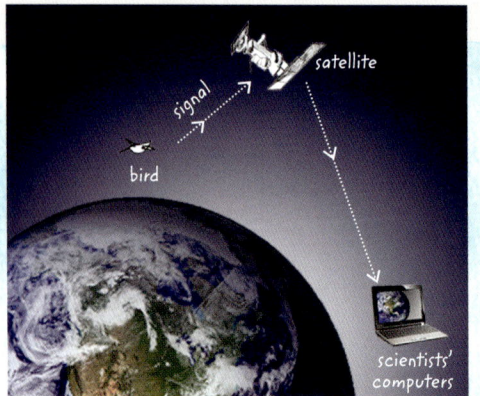

E3 and E7 were tracked by satellite telemetry. Their transmitters sent signals to National Oceanic and Atmospheric Administration (NOAA) polar-orbiting satellites. The satellites in turn bounced the signals to the scientists, who later shared them with the world on the internet (more satellites!).

The NOAA satellites' main function is keeping an eye on the weather but they also do a lot of other things — including following wildlife.

E3 was not the only godwit at the centre. There were three other males and four females. The males were all given backpacks, just like E3. But the females were treated very differently.

Female godwits are larger than males, so instead of backpacks carrying *solar-powered* transmitters, each female had an operation and a *battery-powered* transmitter was inserted into her body.

One of the females was called E7. Just like E3, she was weighed and measured and photographed.

No one knew how important she was going to become.

E7 just after her operation. The transmitter aerial is poking out of her tail feathers.
Photo: Keith Woodley

E3's solar-powered transmitter was exactly the same as the one on this South Island male. 
Photo: Nils Warnock

The transmitters are called PTTs (Platform Terminal Transmitters).

E3's PTT was a mini-solar panel. It weighed 10.5 grams.

E7's PTT was powered by a battery. It weighed 26 grams.

Sun-power!

The PTTs were not programmed to signal all the time.

E3's PTT transmitted for 10 hours then recharged for 48.

E7's PTT transmitted for six hours then rested for 36.

That made waiting for calls all the more nail-biting.

Later that evening, the scientists drove the godwits back to the shore and set them free.

Up they went, back to the flock, back to the sky and the sea.

Altogether 16 godwits were tagged with transmitters. Eight were from Miranda in the North Island and eight were from Golden Bay in the South Island. Eight were males and eight were females.

How can you identify birds when they all look the same?

Researchers mainly use leg bands but they also use flags. Records are kept to say when and where a bird was caught and what shape it was in.

Some bands are metal with ID numbers and others are coloured plastic. The combinations of colours, which leg and which part of the leg form a complex identification code.

Birds with white flags, for instance, are from the North Island of New Zealand, and birds with green flags above the white are from the South Island.

Birds with black flags are super-special: these birds carry transmitters.

The system relies on people reporting bands and flags whenever they see them so that information can be added to the records.

You can help! See page 38 to find out how.

For three more weeks E3 stayed at Miranda. Sometimes he roosted in the pond with the other godwits but, mostly, because he was scared of being caught again, he stayed near the shell bank.

Every day, twice a day, when the sea drew back from the shore, he went to the tidal flats to feed. He ate and ate, and as he ate, the fat piled on and the straps on his backpack tightened. He was humungous.

All the godwits were the same. They were storing energy for the long flight ahead.

Breeding godwits gain and lose huge amounts of weight every year.

Like jets that fly thousands of miles without stopping, they carry their fuel with them. In the case of the birds, it's not jet fuel but fat — over half their body weight (up to 55%).

In the months before they leave, male godwits fatten up from 300 grams to 500 and females from 350 to 600. They have exactly the right amount to get to their next refuelling station.

Their heart and flight muscles become enlarged and their other organs shrink so they are carrying no unnecessary baggage.

You can see how plump this godwit is. No wonder they were once eaten as game birds! They have been protected since 1941.

They were as excited as children at a party. When one flew into the air, the others immediately rose up to join it and suddenly the sky was full of the sight and calls of thousands of birds turning like a scarf flung in the wind.

It was as if they were afraid to be left behind but really they were preparing for the day when they would take off and not come back.

The scientists were excited too. They were still watching the godwits on the beaches through their telescopes but now they had the extra-special birds to keep an eye on. E3's transmitter was sending information to their computers. They knew exactly what he was up to.

That is how they knew when he left.

Next to fuel, the other absolutely crucial thing for the godwits is the state of their feathers or plumage.

Feathers wear out in sunlight and on long trips so, over summer in New Zealand, the birds grow a completely new set. The feathers must be in top condition before the birds depart. Like all birds, godwits constantly clean, smooth and oil their feathers.

Primaries are longest and usually darkest. They are the VIFF (very important flight feathers). When a bird is caught, it is these feathers that are checked to see whether they have been replaced.

On 17 March 2007, E3 and 70 other godwits wheeled and called and wheeled again, and then they were off on one of the most extraordinary journeys in the world.

If you had been on the beach you would have watched them fly up until they were so high you could not see them any more. They were almost two kilometres above the Earth.

They travelled northwest around the edge of the Pacific Ocean, heading for the Yellow Sea.

The routes migrating birds travel are known as flyways. There are eight major flyways in different parts of the world, some of them overlapping.

Godwits from New Zealand fly north along the East Asian-Australasian flyway and return along the West Pacific flyway.

The birds cross the borders of a great many countries but, of course, they don't worry about passports and visas. All they care about are places to eat, roost and nest.

The *East Asian-Australasian* flyway includes 22 countries and is home to over 50 million migratory waterbirds.

They flew by day and they flew by night. They could not land on the water, they could not stop for a drink, they could not stop to eat, they could not stop to sleep. They could not even glide. They just kept flying.

Wing-flap after wing-flap after wing-flap, as regular as your beating heart, they crossed the sea high in the sky.

The godwits' average speed on this trip was about 56 kilometres an hour, just a bit faster than traffic around town, but this can vary a lot depending on conditions. With a tail wind, they can get up to 70 or even 80 km/hr. Nearly open-road speed!

Like most migrating birds the godwits fly in a V-pattern, taking turns to go at the front where it is hardest to push against the air.

Their first stop-over or staging post was the Yellow Sea, a flight of over 10,000 kilometres.

But something was wrong!

E3 was working harder than the other birds and burning his fat too quickly. He was running out of fuel.

Far below, the ocean stretched from horizon to horizon.

He was slowly dropping lower.

He could not land on the sea because he could not swim, and he could not float because he was not waterproof.

The waves were getting closer. He could see little white tips and the sun's sparkle on the water.

It was looking bad, very bad indeed.

Thousands of kilometres away, in New Zealand and in other places around the world, the scientists watched and waited.

Every 48 hours E3's transmitter called their computers and they marked his progress with dots and lines on a globe.

He started well. First he flew north into the Pacific and then he turned northwest, in the direction of the Yellow Sea.

But then, unexpectedly, he landed on the south coast of Papua New Guinea. "Hmm," said the scientists. "What's up, E3?"

They waited 48 hours. In came E3's signal: it was good news and bad news. He had crossed the island and was flying north again. That was good, but he had also flown slightly east, and that was odd.

"Hmm, double-hmm," said the scientists. They scratched their heads.

Another 48 hours passed. In came E3's signal.

"Uh-oh," said the scientists. E3 had flown *south*. Was he returning to New Zealand?

No! His next call was a complete surprise. E3 had flown to Australia.

This was not supposed to happen!

The scientists were dismayed and puzzled.

But it got worse.

What did the silence mean? There were so many possibilities.
— Had E3's solar panel stopped working? Perhaps it had been too cloudy for his transmitter to charge, or maybe it had developed a fault.
— Had his backpack straps loosened and tangled his legs?
— Had he drowned?
— Had he been shot, or eaten by a predator?

E3 missed his next call, and then the next.
Day after day the scientists checked their computers.
"E3! CALL HOME!" commanded Gillian.
But he had gone off-line. He had disappeared in northern Queensland.
They might never see him again.

It was possible that E3 had been devoured by a saltie. Saltwater (or estuarine) crocodiles hang out in river mouths, estuaries, lagoons and swamps along the coast of northern Australia — the same places as wading birds.

They are the largest of all crocodilians and reptiles and will eat anything that enters their territory — including birds, if they can catch them.

E3 would hardly have been worth the effort!

It was a completely different story for E7. She also left Miranda on 17 March but unlike E3, she did not stop at Papua New Guinea. She flew over 10,000 kilometres to the Yalu Jiang estuary on the edge of the Yellow Sea.

It took her seven days and nine hours. She was so exhausted when she landed she could hardly stand up.

For six weeks she ate and rested. She was getting ready for the next stage of her journey, a 6500 kilometre flight to Alaska.

Construction at Donggang on the Yalu River (west), 40 kilometres south of Dandong City.

The Yellow Sea is a shallow sea alongside China, North Korea and South Korea. (There's a map on page 38.) It is a major staging post for hundreds of thousands of migratory birds on the East Asia–Australasian flyway.

There are almost 20,000 square kilometres of inter-tidal flats to feed on. That seems an awful lot but the birds share them with an enormous, hungry, growing human population. Tidal flats are being taken for buildings, farms, roads and airfields, leaving the birds nowhere to recover from their long trip north and nowhere to prepare for the next leg of their journey.

That's what happened at Saemangeum, 270 kilometres southwest of Seoul. In 2006, a 33 kilometre long seawall, the longest in the world, was completed across the Saemangeum estuary, destroying 400 square kilometres of top wading-bird habitat. The wall was especially bad news for two critically-endangered species, the spoon-billed sandpiper and Nordmann's greenshank, both of which relied on Saemangeum as a refuelling stop. The future is not looking good for them.

Spoon-billed sandpiper

Spoon-billed sandpipers are small birds with bills shaped like — a spoon! Like the Nordmann's greenshank, there are fewer than 1000 of these birds left. They nest in northeast Russia and migrate as far south as Bangladesh and Myanmar in the northern winter.

On 2 May, E7 took to the air again. Six non-stop days and one hour later, tired and thin, she touched down.

She had arrived in Alaska in spring, when the frozen tundra explodes into a feast of flying, buzzing, humming life. She had flown 16,800 kilometres for this food, because it would enable her to breed.

And that's just what she did. In the next two months she mated and laid four eggs, and she and her mate raised four healthy young godwits.

In all that time, her transmitter signalled her whereabouts to the watching scientists. They were increasingly surprised and impressed. They had not expected her batteries to last so long.

The tundra in spring is a giant food-store bursting with insect life such as two-winged craneflies.

E7 flew to the central Yukon-Kuskokwim delta (there's a map on page 38) where she mated and laid four pointy brown-speckled eggs in a well-hidden cup-shaped nest on the ground among the lichen and grass.

She and her mate took turns to sit on the eggs for 20–21 days until they hatched. The birds were very stubborn and would not move, even if someone was nearly standing on them!

The chicks were on the go and fed

Photo: Adrian Riegen

themselves from Day One, when their parents showed them where to find food. During this time there was great danger that they would be eaten — by foxes, sandhill cranes, skuas or mink.

But let's say that E7's chicks survived. They could fly by about 29 days, and soon after, in late July, E7 and her mate took off, leaving the young birds on their own.

E7 returned to the coast and joined large flocks of birds feeding up large on clams, worms, seeds and berries around the islands and estuaries. She was preparing for her marathon flight back to New Zealand.

About two months later the young birds followed. They flew across the Pacific without adult guidance. How did they know where to go? That is one of the mysteries of the universe!

At the end of August E7 took off again. This time she flew direct, 11,700 kilometres across the Pacific back to New Zealand. And all the time, her transmitter continued to signal.

By now, the word was out. Something remarkable was happening. Millions followed her progress on the internet.

It was not that she was doing anything different from any other migrating godwit, but it was the first time humans knew all about it. Everyone was very excited. E7 was a superstar. She was on TV and in newspapers right around the world. Some reporters nicknamed her Miranda.

The Daily Bird

September 2007

Record flight confirmed

Watchers around the world have been amazed by the proof that a bar-tailed godwit named 'E7' has flown non-stop for more than 11,700km, travelling from Alaska to Miranda in only eight days.

Although this marathon flight was anticipated by some, it has only now been confirmed.

Astonishingly, E7 has broken her own record, established in March, when she flew over 10,000 km from New Zealand to the Yellow Sea in the first leg of her migration. Altogether, she has been shown to have flown nearly 30,000 km in less than nine months. During this time, she has also nested and, with luck, raised four chicks.

We know about this feat thanks to satellite technology and a tiny transmitter with a battery that exceeded all expectations.

The transmitter, which was implanted in E7's body in February, not only survived the journey north and the months of chick-rearing on the tundra, it continued to transmit throughout her flight south. The signals were weakening and scientists feared that they might fail just prior to her arrival but were ecstatic when her last weak signals were sent from a spot in the mangroves south of Miranda. E7 was clearly in no hurry to face the cameras.

E7, back on the tidal flats at Miranda: 'It's nothing. I do it every year.'

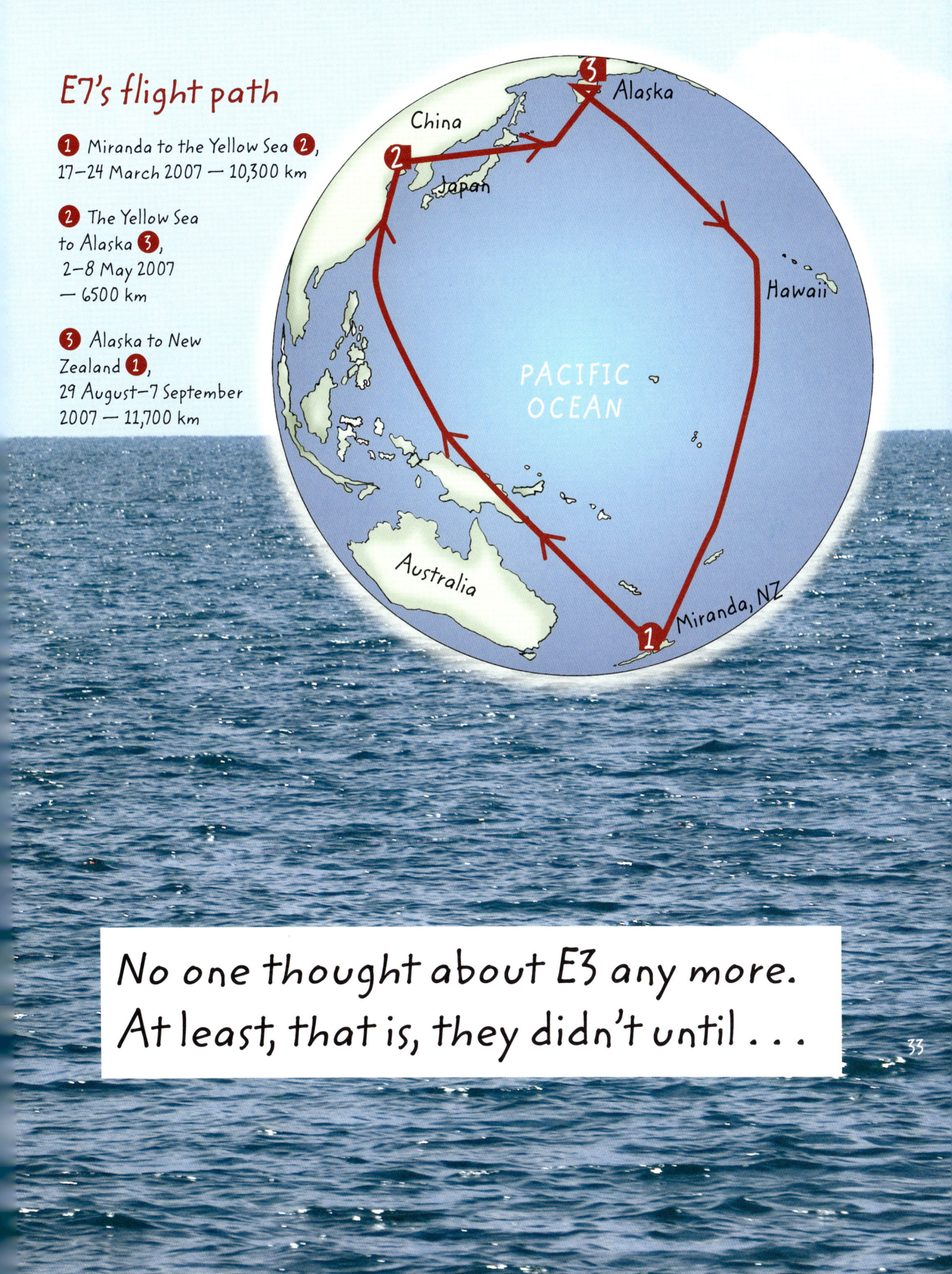

. . . one day six months later.

Gillian was checking the birds at Miranda. She peered through her 'scope at godwits, knots, oystercatchers, wrybills and dotterels. The tide pushed them towards the shore. The sun gleamed on the water. It was a beautiful day.

"Oi!" she said suddenly.

She rubbed her eyes. She looked again.

A male godwit with a black flag on his leg was pottering in the water below the hide. Sometimes he caught worms deep in the mud, sometimes he stretched his wings, preened his feathers, sometimes he dozed on one leg.

Yes, it was E3.

He had flown from Australia and was looking very healthy. He had lost his expensive backpack — but no one really minded.

They were delighted to see him.

E3 was home.

E3 update

'Home' for any creature is the place where it breeds, so technically, for E3, that's Alaska. However, because juvenile godwits spend three to four non-breeding years in the southern hemisphere, and because adult godwits spend six months of every year there as well, there is a strong case for saying that they have two homes and in E3's case, one is New Zealand.

Why did he stop migrating and go to Australia? The answer lay, of course, in his backpack. The solar-powered transmitter was a great idea but came with problems that, in the end, outweighed its advantages. None of the males with these transmitters had a normal migration in 2007 because it is likely that the transmitters interfered with airflow over the body and reduced flying efficiency. The harness fell off when E3 lost weight.

E3 was not at all harmed by his experience and continues to live a godwitly life back on the flyway. He has not been seen in Queensland again. It is likely, because he was not spotted at Miranda from late March until October 2008, that he has resumed normal migration and breeding: he was last seen in April 2009 in Taiwan, again making his way north.

And E7? It is thought that she made the round trip again in 2008 but as of April 2009, she was taking it easy in the estuary at Maketu in the Bay of Plenty.

The godwit tracking project using transmitters is over but that is not the end for the birders. All along the flyway, they continue to band, flag, spot and argue for greater protection for the birds. It's a never-ending story.

E3 hanging out with non-breeding godwits, Queensland, 2007.

E3 in Taiwan, April 2009.

Why are researchers so interested in where the birds go?

The outbreak of H5N1 bird influenza in Asia in January 2004 raised the possibility that the virus might be spread by wild birds as they moved around the world, and in particular, that godwits might carry it from Asia to Alaska. That is why the United States Geological Survey (USGS) and Point Reyes Bird Observatory Conservation Science (PRBO Conservation Science) established and funded a partnership with New Zealand scientists at Massey University. They needed to know more about the godwits' flightpath.

So although the catalyst for the research was the bird 'flu, we also learned a lot more about godwits and that is important too, just for their own sakes. Throughout the East Asian-Australasian flyway, shorebird populations are falling. Staging sites around the Yellow Sea are damaged, polluted and disappearing and, as if that were not enough, conditions in lands on the edge of the Arctic circle are worsening as the tundra warms and thaws. The long-term outlook for birds like the godwits is grim.

Best of all, perhaps, the research has gifted us an increased awareness of the sheer magic of the godwits' lives — how their bodies prepare for migration, how they 'know' when to leave, how they navigate across vast expanses of ocean. How do juvenile godwits, at only a few months old, find their way across the Pacific without adult guidance? We can only marvel at the way in which these birds are so utterly keyed to the rhythms of our world.

Bands and flags

If you find a banded bird or are interested in helping to spot and report bands and flags, check out www.osnz.org.nz/nzwaderstudy.htm or www.doc.org.nz

Hello godwits

The city of Christchurch has taken the godwits to heart. Its citizens have a special farewell ceremony when the birds depart in early March and ring the cathedral bells to welcome them home from late August to early September. It is a sign that spring is on the doorstep.

As scarce as hen's teeth

Were early Māori puzzled by the lack of godwit eggs and chicks? They must have wondered where the birds went for half the year. They asked, "Who has seen the nest of the kūaka?" and when something was lost they said, "It's as hard to find as a kūaka's egg."

How many?

Even though it's hard to be precise and different people quote different figures, the population of New Zealand godwits is thought to be around 75,000. That's down from 100,000 only about ten years ago.

Where they go, where they come from

Ⓐ Yalu Jiang National Nature Reserve
Ⓑ Saemangeum

Ⓒ Yukon-Kuskokwim delta

Find out more

The internet is one of the best places for up-to-date information about migratory birds. Some of the most important organisations and sites are:

Miranda Naturalists' Trust www.miranda-shorebird.org.nz

Ornithological Society of New Zealand www.osnz.org.nz

US Geological Survey http://alaska.usgs.gov/science/biology/shorebirds

PRBO Conservation Science www.prbo.org

Birds Korea www.birdskorea.org

East Asian–Australasian Flyway www.eaaflyway.net

Birdlife International www.birdlife.org

Australasian Wader Studies Group www.awsg.org.au/flagging.php

Department of Conservation www.doc.govt.nz

Forest & Bird www.forestandbird.org.nz

National Wetland Trust www.wetlandtrust.org.nz

You will also readily find many excellent general books about New Zealand birds in your library. For specialist books about godwits, look out Sandra Morris' *Godwit's Journey* and, for grown-ups, the definitive godwit book is *Godwits: Long-haul Champions* by Keith Woodley.

Thanks

The men and women who dedicate their lives to migratory birds are an international team, working together in often hostile and uncomfortable environments. I am in awe of their achievements and their generosity, and acknowledge their unstintingly offered information and photographs. Their contributions have lifted this book to a new level. Robert Gill, Adrian Riegen, Keith Woodley, Phil Battley, Rob Schuckard, Tony Harbraken, ChungYu Chiang, Mei-Yun Tsa, Jesse Conklin, Nial Moores, Nils Warnock and Dorothy Pashniak — thank you.

Early this year I attended the annual Miranda Naturalists' Trust field course and am indebted to its excellent tutors and helpers — Eila Lawton, Dick Veitch, David Melville, Peter Maddison, Keith Thompson, Bill Brownell, Stephen Davies, Gillian Vaughan, Janelle Ward and Audrie McKenzie as well as my fellow students. It was a great week and the ultimate privilege was assisting in capturing, banding and flagging birds, including godwits and their smaller migratory fellows, the red knots.

My appreciation also to those close to home, my family, friends, neighbours and the Random House publishing team: you are too many to name but in the words of my high school principal *you know who you are*.

Special thanks, as always, to Peter Haines, Elwyn Hunt and Jenny Hellen.

Index

A
Alaska 5, 23, 28, 30, 33, 36, 38
Arctic 37
Australasia 28, 37
Australia 26, 27, 36

B
backpack — see transmitter
bands 16, 19, 38
bird-catching 14
bird-watching 12–13

C
cathedral bells 38
chicks 30–31
Christchurch 38
crocodile 27

D
dotterel, New Zealand 11

F
fat 20, 24
feathers 8–9, 10, 16, 17, 21
flags 16, 19, 38
flyway, East Asian-Australasian 22, 28, 37
flyways 22
food for godwits 7

H
H5N1 bird influenza 37
habitat 6–7, 28–29, 30, 36, 37
harness 16, 36
heron, white-faced 10
hide 12, 13, 34

J
juvenile godwits 36, 37

K
kingfisher 9
knot, red 11

L
life list 13

M
Miranda 6–7, 18, 20, 23, 28, 33, 34, 36, 39
Miranda Shorebird Centre 15, 16, 39
mist net 14–15

N
National Oceanic and Atmospheric Administration (NOA) 16
New Zealand 5, 6, 10, 11, 19, 21, 22, 32, 33, 36, 37, 38
New Zealand dotterel 11
Nordmann's greenshank 29

O
oystercatcher 10

P
Pacific Ocean 4, 15, 22, 32

Papua New Guinea 26
pied stilt 11
population 28, 29, 37, 38

R
red knot 11

S
Saemangeum 29, 38
satellite telemetry 16
solar panel 16, 17, 26, 36
speed 23
spoon-billed sandpiper 29
stilt, pied 11

T
telescope 12, 21
transmitter 16, 17, 18, 21, 26, 30, 32, 34, 36
transmitter, battery-powered 17
transmitter, solar-powered 17, 36
tundra 30, 37

W
weight 17, 20, 36
white-faced heron 10
wrybill 11

Y
Yalu Jiang 28, 29, 38
Yalu River 28
Yellow Sea 22, 23, 28, 29, 33, 37
Yukon-Kuskokwim delta 30, 38

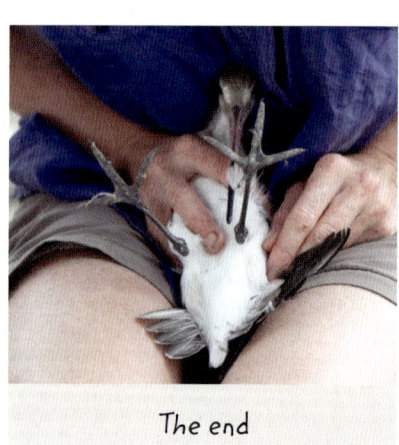

The end